LEARN STUFF UNKNOWN & TICKLE YOUR FUNNY BONE WHILE SITTING ON THE THROWN

WRITTEN & CREATED BY
LOU FLUSHER

WE UNDERSTAND THAT LIFE'S MOST PROFOUND THOUGHTS OFTEN OCCUR WHEN SEATED IN SOLITARY SPLENDOR, SO WHY NOT EQUIP YOURSELF WITH A DELIGHTFUL DOSE OF TRIVIA AND CHUCKLES? AFTER ALL, IT'S ONLY NATURAL TO SEEK ENLIGHTENMENT IN THE MIDST OF YOUR DAILY... UH, ROUTINE.

WE PROMISE A COLLECTION OF FACTS AND TALES THAT ARE AS FASCINATING AS THEY ARE UNEXPECTED. FROM ASTONISHING HISTORICAL ANECDOTES TO MIND–BOGGLING SCIENTIFIC TRIVIA, CONSIDER THIS YOUR VIP PASS TO THE INTELLECTUAL AND COMEDIC WONDERS OF THE TOILET WORLD. AS WELL AS SOME STRAIGHT FORWARD TOILET HUMOUR.

AS YOU'RE SEATED AND READY TO MAKE HISTORY (OR AT LEAST READ ABOUT IT), LET'S DIVE HEADFIRST INTO THIS DELIGHTFUL DIVE OF DIVERSION. RELAX, RELEASE, AND REVEL IN THE RIVETING REALM OF RANDOM REVELATIONS. AND HEY, IF SOMEONE ASKS WHAT TOOK YOU SO LONG, JUST TELL THEM YOU WERE SOLVING THE WORLD'S MYSTERIES—ONE FLUSH AT A TIME.

CONTENTS

POOP CHECKLIST

- ☑ **READING MATERIAL:** DO YOU HAVE ADEQUATE READING MATERIAL, BE IT A BOOK, MAGAZINE, OR SMARTPHONE?

- ☐ **TIME MANAGEMENT:** HAVE YOU CALCULATED THE OPTIMAL AMOUNT OF TIME TO SPEND WITHOUT LOSING FEELING IN YOUR LEGS?

- ☐ **AMBIANCE:** IS THE BATHROOM PROPERLY STOCKED WITH AIR FRESHENER OR MATCHES FOR POST-POOP AMBIANCE CONTROL?

- ☐ **EMERGENCY EXIT:** IS THERE AN ESCAPE PLAN IN CASE SOMEONE STARTS JIGGLING THE DOORKNOB?

- ☐ **SOUNDTRACK:** DID YOU PICK THE RIGHT PLAYLIST OR PODCAST TO ACCOMPANY YOUR CONTEMPLATIVE MOMENTS?

- ☐ **PHONE PLACEMENT:** IS YOUR PHONE WITHIN REACH, BUT NOT IN DANGER OF BEING DROPPED INTO THE ABYSS?

- ☐ **TOILET PAPER SUPPLY:** HAVE YOU ENSURED A COMFORTABLE AND SUFFICIENT SUPPLY OF TOILET PAPER?

- ☐ **MINDFUL MEDITATION:** ARE YOU READY TO PONDER LIFE'S MYSTERIES, LIKE WHY THE SHOWER THOUGHTS ARE ALWAYS SO PROFOUND?

- ☐ **AVOIDING DISTRACTIONS:** ARE YOU COMMITTED TO IGNORING RANDOM NOTIFICATIONS AND INSTEAD ENJOYING YOUR MOMENT OF PEACE?

FART JOKES

What did one fart say to the other at the party?
"Let's blow this joint!"

Why don't scientists trust farts?
They're too full of hot air!

Did you hear about the fart that won an award?
It was a real "stinker"!

Why did the fart go to therapy?
It had some "deep-seated" issues!

Why don't farts play hide and seek?
They're always caught!

What's a fart's favorite superhero power? *The ability to "clear the room"!*

Why did the fart apply for a job?
It wanted to make some "cents"!

Did you hear about the fart that joined a band?
It was the "wind" instrument!

What do you call a person who doesn't like fart jokes?
A "party pooper"!

What did one fart say to the other?
"You crack me up!"

Why do farts smell?
So that deaf people can enjoy them too!

Did you hear about the restaurant that only serves beans?
It's always packed – with toots of flavor!

Why don't scientists trust atoms?
Because they make up everything, even farts!

What's a fart's favorite music genre?
Pop!

Did you hear about the gas molecule that won the Nobel Prize?
It was outstanding in its field!

Why don't farts graduate from school?
Because they always get expelled!

What do you call a fart that's had too much sugar?
A "tootie fruity"!

TOILET HUMOUR

Why did the toilet paper roll down the hill?
To get to the bottom, of course!

What's a bathroom's favorite type of music?
Pop!

Why did the toilet paper get thrown out of the party?
Because it was being too clingy!

What did one toilet say to the other?
"You look flushed today!"

Why was the math book sad in the bathroom?
It had too many problems!

What's a toilet's favorite dessert?
Plum pudding, of course!

Why did the smartphone refuse to go to the bathroom?
It was afraid of getting a "cracked" screen!

What did one toilet say to the other in a race?
"I'm feeling flushed with victory!"

Why don't toilets ever get invited to parties?
They always bring up old crap!

Why was the calendar afraid of going to the bathroom?
It feared its days were numbered!

Why did the toilet paper roll down the stairs?
To get to the bottom, where all the action is!

What do you call a bathroom that has no doors?
A good place to let off some steam!

Why was the toilet paper a great comedian?
Because it always knew how to deliver a clean punchline!

What's a toilet's favorite type of music?
Anything with a good "beat"!

Why was the bathroom mirror upset?
It felt like everyone was always reflecting on its appearance!

MIND BLOWING FACTS

Bananas: Bananas are berries, but strawberries are not actually berries. The fruit world is full of identity crises!

Sneezing: Sneezes can travel up to 100 miles per hour. That's like a tiny, unexpected jet engine blast.

Octopuses: Octopuses have three hearts – two to love and one to say, "No, don't eat that!"

Ketchup: In the 1830s, ketchup was sold as medicine. Imagine getting a prescription for a French fry dip!

Giraffes: Giraffes have long necks, but only seven neck vertebrae, just like humans. They've mastered the art of neck elongation with style!

Dolphins: Dolphins give each other names, and they can call each other even when they're not in sight. Imagine dolphins having their version of a name-based roll call!

Velociraptors: Velociraptors were actually only about the size of turkeys. Hollywood really gave them an ego boost!

Pineapples: Pineapples were such a symbol of wealth in 18th century Europe that people would rent them for parties instead of buying them.

Eyes: Your eyes are actually the same size from birth, but your nose and ears never stop growing. Thank goodness our eyes aren't catching up!

Cows: Cows have best friends and can get stressed when they're separated. Moo-ving tales of bovine friendship!

Rainbows: You can never touch a rainbow, but if you try hard enough, you might find a pot of gold at the end. Or just a muddy puddle.

Space: In space, astronauts can't cry properly because their tears won't fall. Tears just might be the only thing gravity has control over.

Vending Machines: Vending machines are twice as likely to kill you as a shark is. Be cautious when you're seeking snacks!

Elephants: Elephants can't jump, but they're great at stomping and trumpeting. Just imagine if they tried to join a basketball game!

Cats: The world's oldest known pet cat was found in a 9,500-year-old grave on the Mediterranean island of Cyprus. Cats have been ruling for a long time!

Platypuses: The male platypus has venomous spurs on its back legs. Just when you thought platypuses couldn't get any more bizarre!

Honey: Honey never spoils. Archaeologists have found pots of honey in ancient Egyptian tombs that are over 3,000 years old and still perfectly edible.

Snails: Some snails can sleep for up to three years. Now that's some serious snoozing!

Time Dilation: If you were to travel at the speed of light for a while and return to Earth, you might find that less time has passed for you than for those who stayed on Earth. This phenomenon, predicted by Einstein's theory of relativity, is known as time dilation.

The Great Emu War: In 1932, Australia had a real war against emus. Farmers were dealing with a population boom of emus damaging their crops. The government deployed soldiers armed with machine guns, but the emus proved elusive and ran faster than expected, leading to a "defeat" for the humans. It's now known as "The Great Emu War."

Abraham Lincoln: Abraham Lincoln was an accomplished wrestler. He was known for his strength and skills in the wrestling ring, and only lost one out of around 300 matches.

Albert Einstein: Einstein's famous equation, $E=mc^2$, doesn't appear in his original papers on relativity. It was a later formulation that summarized his theory of special relativity.

Jim Carrey: wrote himself a check for $10 million for "acting services rendered" before he was famous. He dated it for 10 years in the future and carried it in his wallet. Eventually, he received roles that paid him over $10 million.

Sir Isaac Newton: The famous physicist, once stuck a needle in his eye to test his theories about optics. He inserted the needle between his eye and the bone to observe how it would affect his vision.

T-Rex: Despite its reputation as a fearsome predator, T-Rex's arms were surprisingly tiny, with proportions that would be more fitting for a human child than a massive dinosaur.

Stegosaurus: The Stegosaurus had a second brain in its hips, known as the "second brain," which helped control its hind legs and tail. It's believed this arrangement helped coordinate movement for such a large dinosaur.

Cleopatra: the last pharaoh of Egypt, lived closer in time to the invention of the iPhone than to the construction of the Great Pyramid of Giza.

The Great Wall of China: is not visible from space with the naked eye. This common myth has been debunked by astronauts.

Oxford University: is older than the Aztec Empire. Oxford was founded in the 12th century, while the Aztec Empire began in the 14th century.

The Mammoth: went extinct about 1,000 years after the construction of the Great Pyramid of Giza. It survived longer than most people realize.

Computer Bug: The first recorded "computer bug" was a literal bug – a moth – that caused a malfunction in Harvard's Mark II computer in 1947.

Anglo-Zanzibar War: The shortest war in history lasted just 38 to 45 minutes. It was the Anglo-Zanzibar War of 1896 between the United Kingdom and the Sultanate of Zanzibar.

Eiffel Tower: The construction of the Eiffel Tower was completed in just over two years. It was built as the entrance arch for the 1889 World's Fair in Paris.

Ancient Rome: In ancient Rome, public urinals were a common sight. They were placed along streets and were often social spaces for conversation.

Last Emperor of China: The youngest person to ever become a ruler was Puyi, the last Emperor of China, who ascended to the throne at the age of 2 years and 10 months.

Ottoman Empire: The Ottoman Empire spanned three continents (Europe, Asia, and Africa) and lasted for over 600 years, making it one of the longest-lasting empires in history.

Fax Machine: The fax machine was invented in the 19th century. Scottish inventor Alexander Bain created a working prototype in the 1840s.

King Louis XIV: The longest reigning monarch in history is King Louis XIV of France, who reigned for over 72 years.

Urine: Ancient Romans used urine to clean their clothes and bleach their teeth. Urine contains ammonia, which has cleaning properties.

Mount Vesuvius: The eruption of Mount Vesuvius in 79 AD that buried Pompeii also preserved it remarkably well, providing valuable insights into daily life in ancient Rome.

The Library of Alexandria: one of the most famous libraries in history, is believed to have been destroyed in multiple stages rather than a single catastrophic event.

Neutron Star: A teaspoon of a neutron star would weigh about 6 billion tons. Neutron stars are incredibly dense remnants of massive stars.

Honey: Honey never spoils. Archaeologists have found pots of honey in ancient Egyptian tombs that are over 3,000 years old and still perfectly edible.

Chess: There are more possible iterations of a game of chess than there are atoms in the known universe. That's the power of exponential possibilities!

Venus: A day on Venus is longer than its year. Venus takes about 243 Earth days to complete one rotation, but only about 225 Earth days to orbit the sun.

Paper: If you could fold a piece of paper in half 42 times, it would reach the moon. The exponential growth quickly becomes mind-boggling.

Taste Buds: Your taste buds have a lifespan of about 10 to 14 days. They're constantly regenerating as old ones die off and new ones grow.

Honeybees: can recognize human faces. Researchers have found that bees can associate a picture of a face with a sugary reward.

Mountain Range: The longest mountain range in the world is underwater. The Mid-Ocean Ridge stretches around the globe for more than 40,000 miles.

The closest planet to Earth: Venus, can sometimes be seen in the daytime if you know where to look. It's often called the "Evening Star" or "Morning Star."

Time Dilation: The phenomenon known as "time dilation" occurs at high speeds or in strong gravitational fields, causing time to pass more slowly for an observer in motion compared to one at rest.

Carbon: The average human body contains enough carbon to fill about 9,000 pencils. You're basically a walking collection of carbon atoms!

Space: Sound can't travel through space because it requires a medium (like air, water, or solids) to transmit vibrations.

Brain: Your brain generates enough electrical power to light up a small LED bulb. It's like having a tiny light show inside your head!

Gold: The world's oceans contain an estimated 20 million tons of gold, dissolved in seawater. Unfortunately, it's too dilute to economically extract.

Christopher Walken: Christopher Walken trained as a lion tamer during a circus job early in his career. He has a unique set of skills!

Steve Martin: Steve Martin is an accomplished banjo player. He's even won Grammy Awards for his bluegrass music.

Keanu Reeves: Keanu Reeves gave away a significant portion of his earnings from "The Matrix" trilogy to the special effects and costume design teams, as he believed they deserved it more than he did.

Brad Pitt: Brad Pitt worked as an El Pollo Loco mascot while trying to make it as an actor. He danced around in a chicken suit to attract customers.

Sylvester Stallone: Sylvester Stallone was homeless and sold his dog for $50 before making it big with "Rocky." After his success, he bought his dog back for $3,000.

Walt Disney: Walt Disney was afraid of mice, despite creating one of the most iconic mice characters in history – Mickey Mouse.

Marilyn Monroe: Marilyn Monroe had an IQ of 168, which is considered highly intelligent. She was not just a glamorous star but also quite intellectually capable.

Michael Jackson: Michael Jackson tried to buy Marvel Comics in the 1990s just to play the role of Spider-Man in his own produced film.

J.K. Rowling: J.K. Rowling wrote parts of the "Harry Potter" series on napkins, and the initial idea for the series came to her during a train ride.

Trees: There are more trees on Earth than stars in the Milky Way galaxy. Estimates suggest there are around 3 trillion trees on our planet.

Earth: The Earth isn't a perfect sphere; it's slightly flattened at the poles and slightly bulging at the equator due to its rotation

Starquakes: There's a phenomenon called "starquakes," where the interior of a star vibrates like a struck bell. This helps astronomers learn more about the star's internal structure.

Boötes Void: There's a region in space called the "Boötes Void" where very few galaxies exist. It's about 330 million light-years in diameter and appears nearly empty.

Uranus: rotates almost on its side, with its rotational axis tilted nearly 98 degrees. It's essentially rolling along its orbital path.

Saturn: Saturn's rings aren't solid; they're made up of countless chunks of ice and rock ranging in size from grains of sand to small mountains.

QUIZ

ANSWERS ARE ON PAGE 69

QUESTION 1: WHICH COUNTRY HAS A MUSEUM DEDICATED TO CARROTS?

A) AUSTRALIA
B) UNITED KINGDOM
C) JAPAN
D) NETHERLANDS

QUESTION 2: WHAT IS THE OFFICIAL ANIMAL OF SCOTLAND?

A) HIGHLAND COW
B) LOCH NESS MONSTER
C) UNICORN
D) HAGGIS

QUESTION 3: WHAT IS THE FEAR OF LONG WORDS CALLED?

A) HIPPOPOTOMONSTROSESQUIPEDALIOPHOBIA
B) ARACHNOPHOBIA
C) CLAUSTROPHOBIA
D) ACROPHOBIA

QUESTION 4: IN WHICH COUNTRY IS IT ILLEGAL TO NAME YOUR CHILD "BRFXXCCXXMNPCCCCLLLMMNPRXVCLMNCKSS QLBB11116"?

A) SWEDEN
B) ICELAND
C) DENMARK
D) NORWAY

QUESTION 5: WHICH ANIMAL IS KNOWN AS THE "SHIP OF THE DESERT"?

A) CAMEL
B) ELEPHANT
C) OSTRICH
D) LLAMA

QUESTION 6: WHAT IS THE NATIONAL SPORT OF BHUTAN?

A) SOCCER
B) ARCHERY
C) CRICKET
D) SUMO WRESTLING

QUESTION 7: WHICH PLANET IS KNOWN AS THE "RED PLANET"?

A) VENUS
B) MARS
C) JUPITER
D) SATURN

QUESTION 8: HOW MANY BONES ARE THERE IN AN ADULT HUMAN BODY?

A) 126
B) 206
C) 312
D) 452

QUESTION 9: WHICH COUNTRY HAS A FLOATING POST OFFICE?

A) MALDIVES
B) JAPAN
C) CANADA
D) ITALY

QUESTION 10: WHAT IS THE TERM FOR A GROUP OF FLAMINGOS?

A) FLOCK
B) HERD
C) FLAMBOYANCE
D) TROOP

QUESTION 11: HOW MANY TIME ZONES DOES CHINA OFFICIALLY HAVE?

A) 1
B) 2
C) 3
D) 1 WITH VARIATIONS

QUESTION 12: IN WHICH COUNTRY CAN YOU FIND THE GREAT BARRIER REEF?

A) AUSTRALIA
B) BRAZIL
C) INDONESIA
D) INDIA

QUESTION 13: WHAT IS THE SMALLEST BONE IN THE HUMAN BODY?

A) FEMUR
B) TIBIA
C) STAPES
D) RADIUS

QUESTION 14: WHAT IS THE NATIONAL SPORT OF JAPAN?

A) JUDO
B) SUMO WRESTLING
C) KARATE
D) BASEBALL

QUESTION 15: WHICH COUNTRY HOLDS AN
ANNUAL "MONKEY BUFFET FESTIVAL"?

A) THAILAND
B) INDIA
C) CHINA
D) BRAZIL

QUESTION 16: WHAT IS THE NAME FOR A GROUP
OF CROWS?

A) GANG
B) MURDER
C) FLOCK
D) COVEN

QUESTION 17: IN WHICH CITY IS THE FAMOUS LEANING TOWER LOCATED?

A) PARIS
B) ROME
C) PISA
D) ATHENS

QUESTION 18: WHICH ANIMAL HAS FINGERPRINTS SIMILAR TO HUMANS?

A) DOLPHINS
B) KOALAS
C) ELEPHANTS
D) GORILLAS

QUESTION 19: HOW MANY LEGS DOES A SPIDER TYPICALLY HAVE?

A) 6
B) 8
C) 10
D) 12

QUESTION 20: WHICH ANIMAL CAN SLEEP FOR UP TO THREE YEARS?

A) KOALA
B) ELEPHANT
C) SNAIL
D) BAT

RIDDLES

THE MORE YOU TAKE, THE MORE
YOU LEAVE BEHIND.
WHAT AM I?

FOOTSTEPS

30

I SPEAK WITHOUT A MOUTH AND HEAR WITHOUT EARS. I HAVE NO BODY, BUT I COME ALIVE WITH THE WIND.
WHAT AM I?

ECHO

I HAVE KEYS BUT OPEN NO LOCKS. I HAVE SPACE BUT NO ROOM. YOU CAN ENTER BUT NOT GO OUTSIDE.
WHAT AM I?

PIANO

THE MAN WHO INVENTED IT DOESN'T WANT IT. THE MAN WHO BOUGHT IT DOESN'T NEED IT. THE MAN WHO NEEDS IT DOESN'T KNOW IT.
WHAT IS IT?

I CAN FLY WITHOUT WINGS, CRY WITHOUT EYES. WHEREVER I GO, DARKNESS FOLLOWS ME. WHAT AM I?

CLOUD

I CAN BE CRACKED, MADE, TOLD, AND PLAYED.
WHAT AM I?

I'M LIGHT AS A FEATHER, YET
THE STRONGEST PERSON CAN'T
HOLD ME FOR MUCH LONGER
THAN A MINUTE.
WHAT AM I?

I'M NOT ALIVE, BUT I CAN GROW;
I DON'T HAVE LUNGS, BUT I NEED
AIR; I DON'T HAVE A MOUTH, BUT
WATER KILLS ME.
WHAT AM I?

FIRE

I SPEAK WITHOUT A MOUTH AND HEAR WITHOUT EARS. I HAVE NO BODY, BUT I COME ALIVE WITH THE WIND.
WHAT AM I?

AIR

I AM TAKEN FROM A MINE, AND SHUT UP IN A WOODEN CASE, FROM WHICH I AM NEVER RELEASED, AND YET I AM USED BY ALMOST EVERY PERSON. WHAT AM I?

GAMES

STILL POOING? OK THESE GAMES WILL KEEP YOU OCCUPIED AND PROVIDE AMPLE EXCUSE FOR WHY YOU'RE TAKING SO LONG.

THE ANSWERS TO ALL THE GAMES ARE ON PAGES 70 – 74

```
C H A J E E D G O Y B F O B
P L X P S F L O A T E R S O
A E Z A O K G L Y D P I N O
B R E Y U O E L Z O I S W L
G T O W G I P P Y O D J E Y
R E W S A M H I W D U C T I
O T Q E G U Y S E O S P S V
S I R K E E M S X O F S E T
S G U P A W Y T C A U T A V
D Y R S Q E E W R S K U T A
Q U I N T S F E A R I N L N
U C N O Y I J G P B A K E Y
R K E H E V N S H I T N P A
I Y O U S S O K C M S J T H
```

PEE	POOP	STINK
PISS	SHIT	STUNK
URINE	CRAP	GROSS
WEEWEE	DOODOO	YUCKY
WETSEAT	FLOATERS	GAG

MAZES
1

5

SUDOKU

GRID - 1

Hard

		9			5		8	
	1	8	2				5	3
5	6			9	8			
2		6				5	7	
						1	6	
1			6					8
7			1	5	4	8	3	6
	5	1		3			4	9
	4	3		2		7		5

GRID - 2

Hard

8		9		4	5			
		7	1	8	3			
			9			4	8	1
	8			3	6	5		
3	6		5	9			7	
1			2		8			4
9			7	6	4	3	5	
6		3	8					
4			3				9	6

GRID - 3

Hard

	4					1	6	5
1	6	7	5		9			
	8	3						
4	7	5	8				9	
		1			7			4
	2		4	9	5	3	7	
	1		9	8	6		5	7
	5	8			3			
	9	4		5	2			

GRID - 4

Hard

	4	8	1		6		9	
		6		4				7
			2	3		5		
	1	2	6		3			
	8	5			2	6	3	1
6			4	5			2	
		1			7	4		
9		4		1			8	6
2		3	8			1		9

GRID - 5

Hard

6		4				1	5	
3	5		4					9
8	9		5					6
	8	3			1	5		
7				3				2
4		6	8		9			7
	4	8		7	5	6		1
1	6		9	8	2			5
5		9	1					

GRID - 6

Hard

	9	6		4			1	
1	7					9	4	
3			9	1				5
	5		1	9		8	6	
7		1	3			4	9	
			4					1
	6		7		1		2	4
2		4			9	6		
8	3		6	2		1		

GRID - 7

Hard

	6			8			7	2
	4			9	1	6		8
	1	7						
			3			7	1	
6	3	1			9			
	2	4		6		3	9	
	9		8			5	2	7
4		3	9		2	8	6	
2	8			1		9		

GRID - 8

Hard

	6		9					
2				7				6
4	9		6		5		8	3
5	4	2	3				9	1
7					9	8	3	
	8		4		7			2
				6	2		1	9
			7		4	3	2	8
	2			1	5			7

GRID - 9

Hard

	9	7		1	6		4	5
				8	9	6		
		7						
2		1			8			
9		5	8		4			
6		8	9			2	3	
5	8			9				
4	1	9	3	6		5	7	
7	2		5		8	1		6

GRID - 10

Hard

							2	
	4		7	2			1	9
		2		3	4	7	6	5
4		6			1			
1		7	4				9	2
5	2	8		9	3		7	
9			5					1
2		1			9		4	6
3				4	2		8	

GRID - 11

Hard

8	4				7	5		
5	2	1		3	4		6	9
7		3	2		6			1
4			6	8	2	1	7	3
6				7	3		9	
3			4	9				
		5			8	9		
9			7	6				
2	7		1					6

GRID - 12

Hard

	8	4		6		1		
		1	8				9	7
2	9		3		1			
	4		1	7	6			2
	5	2	4	9	8		6	
8					5		7	
					7		4	5
9		8		4	3	2		
4					2		3	8

GRID - 13

		5	9	8		7		
8	2			6		3		
	7			5			9	1
			6	7		5	8	
5	8		2	9		6		
	6	2	8	4			7	9
		8		2		4		
7	5		4	3				8
2		3		1				5

GRID - 14

				3		8	5	
		8		6				
6	3	5					4	9
1	7			8	9		6	5
	5			7	6	9	8	
8			4	5			7	
		1		3	6	2		
3	2		6	4	8	5		
9	8	6			7		1	

GRID - 15

	6		8	7	5	3	2	1
		1	9		3	4		
7	2							9
		5					3	2
2	3			6				7
	9	7	3	5	2			8
8		6		3		1		
	5	2	6				8	4
					8	2		

GRID - 16

8								
7	5	2	4			1		6
4	6				5	8		9
	9	1	8	3				
3		4			7			
		8	2			3	4	
	3	6		5	2	7	8	
9			1		8	2	6	3
2	8	7		4	3	5		1

GRID - 17

			9	3	7	2	6	
9	7	2	5		6	1		
	6	5			2		9	8
		9				3	7	
		8		6				
2	5	6					8	1
5		7			9			3
	1			7			2	
			2	5	4		1	7

GRID - 18

6			2		4	8	9	
			6		3		1	
2	3					4	5	
1		8	9			7		
		6		2	1			
3	9			4			2	
5	6	2	4	8		3		1
8		3	5	6		9		
	4					6	8	

GRID - 19

			5	9		3		7
9		1						5
	7			6	4	8		9
	5		1		8		3	6
8		7		5				1
4	1				7			2
3			4	2		1		
	9	8	3					4
	4			7		6	9	3

GRID - 20

2					5			
9			1				8	2
7	8				4	1		9
8	9	2	4	6			3	
3	7	1	5					
4	5		2	3		8		1
1	2	7	9					3
	3						1	8
			3	1		9		

GRID - 21

4	8		7	1	5			
					2	5	8	3
						4		
		7				1	4	2
1	6	4	5		9		3	
	2	8	1	4			5	6
2	3			5	4	7		8
			2	7			9	
	7	5	3	8	1	6		4

GRID - 22

9		8			6	2		7
3	4			2		6		
	7	6				4		8
				5				4
	2		4	8		3		
	9		3			8	6	2
7	8	3			2			
1	5	2		3				
	6	9	1			7	2	3

GRID - 23

	3		9	2				8
	9		8		4	5		
		7		5	3			
	8	9	5				1	6
3			7		8	2	9	
2		4		1	9	7		5
		8			7		5	3
		6	2					9
		3	4		1		2	

GRID - 24

				3	4		6	7
3	6	8	5	9	7			
9								
	5	6				7		
8			9	7	5	6	4	
				1		2	3	5
2			4	5		8	7	
	5					4		
6	1		7		2	3	5	9

GRID - 25

Hard

7	6	5						
		4		7		3	1	5
		8	5	4	9			
	2	6	9	1		5	3	8
9	1			4	8		6	
				2		4	9	
	7	9			1			6
8		1				2		
6		2	8			1	7	3

GRID - 26

Hard

			6				8	
2				1	9	3		6
6						1	4	
7	1	6		8	3	5		
8	9	4	1				3	7
3		2	7	9	4			
		3		5	7			
	6		9			8		3
4				2	6	9		

GRID - 27

Hard

	1		2	8	3			
	5			1		3	8	6
	8	7					9	1
	7	5		4		9		
8		9	1			6	4	
4		3	9		5		1	
5	3		4	7		1		
6	9	1				4	7	
7		8			1	5		3

GRID - 28

Hard

3	6		9			1		
4				1		7		
	1	9		7				6
5				8	7			3
	7			5	2			8
	4	2		7		6	1	
		4		8		5	6	
	2			9	6		3	4
	8	5		1		9		7

GRID - 29

Hard

	7	9	8					5
			1	7				
		6	9			3	8	7
				8	4		2	
9	4		3		1	7	5	8
		8	7		2		4	
4			6		8		3	2
	2	5	4				6	
1				5	9		7	

GRID - 30

Hard

8	2	7	1	9				
9	3	4	8					2
		1		3	7		4	9
			5	8				7
	1							
				4	2	3	1	5
1				6	7			3
	4	8	7	2			6	
3	7	6		1	8			

GRID - 31

Hard

2		8		6				9
	6		9			5		2
		5		3				
	7		8	4				5
	3		2		9		6	
			1		3		7	4
	2	6	3	8	1	4		
		3	5	2		6		1
	5		6	9		2	8	

GRID - 32

Hard

	4	6				3	5	8
	5		4	9		2	7	6
		7	6			1		4
		2		7	9	8	4	1
			2			5	3	9
8	9				4		6	
	7					4		
	6	8					2	5
			9	1				7

GRID - 33

Hard

1		6			8	5		
	9	4		2		8		1
	8		1		6			9
3	7				5			8
4	5	8		3	1	6	9	7
			8		4			5
8		7	5			9	2	
9			7	8				
6	2		4		9			3

GRID - 34

Hard

7			4			1		5
5	9	6	8			2		4
		8	3		5		9	
		2	6			5	7	
		5				4		2
		4		8	2		1	
2	5	7		6	3			
	6		2		7			3
4		9			8	6		

GRID - 35

Hard

7	6		5		3	8		2
5					8	1		4
	9	8	4		2	3	5	7
2			8	5		4	3	6
					1	5		
	5	7			6	9		
4	2	1		3		7		
	7			8	4			5
		5	1					3

GRID - 36

Hard

4	8				6	7		9
	2		7	9		3	4	
	9			8	3			
6	3		8	5			1	
	4	2	9		1			
9	5	1	3				7	4
	6			4		5		3
5	7	4		3				
	1	9			8	4		7

GRID - 37

Hard

2	6	1	5		7	9	3	
8		5	3			1	6	
	3	9		1				
	1				3	7	8	
7			1			5	2	
	8			7				
			9		6		4	
	2	3				6	1	
6	4		7	3	1		5	

GRID - 38

Hard

	9	1		7				5
3				6			4	
2		4		8	3		9	6
		7		3			6	4
7				4		2	5	
	6	5				9		7
	1	2					7	9
	6	3		9	7		1	
9			6		8			3

GRID - 39

Hard

8	7	5				4	9	
	4	2	6	8				
			4	9				5
		6			9		8	7
				1		9		
	1		7				4	
5	9	7		4				
2			8		1	6	7	9
6	8		9	7	3		5	4

GRID - 40

Hard

						2		9
	4			8	9	6		
9	2	8		7		1	4	3
		3	7		8			4
		2	4	9		3		
6	9	4		1				8
4		9	3	6		5	7	
5		7					3	6
				5		4		

GRID - 41

Hard

		5			7		1	3
4	9							
			4			9	2	6
		3	1	7	2	6		
		9	6	5	8		4	
5	1			3	4		7	
1		2		4	9	5		8
		7		8		1	6	
		4			1	2		

GRID - 42

Hard

				3	5	4		
5	8						1	3
	7					8		5
8		7			3		2	6
	2			8		5		
6	4	5		9		3		
	3	1			4	6		2
2	5		1	6	9	7		
	6		3			1	5	

GRID - 43

Hard

2		5		9	4			
6	9	4	8					
	7			5				
	6	9				3		
			4	3	9	6	7	
				8	6	9	5	1
3		6	5	4	2			9
		2				1		5
4	5		9		8	2	6	3

GRID - 44

Hard

		9	7				5	
3	4	7		1	5	8	2	
5				8		3	7	
		2	9				6	
	8	5	3		6	4	1	
7		6			8	2	9	
2			8	6				
	9				2	7		
	7				3	6	4	

GRID - 45

Hard

			8		1		6	
6		1		5	7			
		8	6	4				
3						1	4	2
9		7		2	6			
		2	1	3				
4		9	7		3	5	1	8
8	7		9	1	4		3	
1			2	8				9

GRID - 46

Hard

						1	5	
				9	6	8		7
		1			2			6
2	8	1	7	6				9
3		4			1		8	5
9	7	5	3	4	8		1	
6	1		4	5		9		
5	3	9			7			
				1				3

GRID - 47

Hard

						2	9	
	4		1			3	8	
			2					4
9	2		5	8		7		3
		7	3		2			
5					7	1	2	6
		2		9	1	4		
8			7	2	4	5	6	9
	9	4			3	8		2

GRID - 48

Hard

2			7				8	1
	1	7			8	9	5	
9	8				6	7		2
	6	1		2		5	4	3
7		2		6	5		1	9
3			4		1	6		7
				9			7	
	7	4	6		2			
	9		8	7				

GRID - 49

Hard

			1	9	2		4	8
	4			6				
8		2			4			1
			2		6			
6	3	8		1	7			
5		4	9		8			7
2				8	9		3	
3	8	9	6	4	1		5	
4		5	7					6

GRID - 50

Hard

3			4		6			
9		7	1	3	5			
1	4		9		7		6	
		1						
		4		1	3			6
7				5	8	1	9	
		3	8		1	6	5	
6	8		5	7	4		3	
		9		6	2		8	7

GRID - 51

Hard

5				4				
						1	4	7
4			3		2		9	5
7	5		6					3
1	4				8	6	7	
6				3	7		5	
8		4	2					9
2			1	9	4		6	
		7	8		5	3	2	4

GRID - 52

Hard

1			9	7	3	4		
	9		2		8		7	
3			6				9	
5		2	1	3	4	6		
9	3	4	8			7		5
6	8							4
	4			6		8		
	1	5				3		6
8			4		1			7

GRID - 53

Hard

	2	9	4	6		3		
	3	6		5	1			
1							5	
9	5				7	2	8	6
		8	1	2	9	7		
	4	7		8	6	9	3	1
	1	2	8			5		
4		3		1			6	2
	7			3	2			

GRID - 54

Hard

			5		2		6	8
		2		6				7
8					4	2		1
5		9	4	8		7		
6	8	3	7	2		4		5
	2	4				8		6
2	4		6	3		1		
3		8			9			
					7	6		2

GRID - 55

8	5			1	7		3	4
	7	2			3			
4		1	8					5
	4	3		7	1	8		2
				8	2	4		6
		8	6	4		7		
3	8			6				
	1	7		3	8			
2			1		5			7

GRID - 56

			3	4	8			
			2		9		6	
4				6	5			
7				5		4	1	
6		5					8	7
		8	4	9		6		
9	7	4	6		1			
5	8	6	9	3		7		1
	3	1		7			9	6

GRID - 57

		4		1		8	9	2
	3		4	8		1	7	6
		1				5		
1	5		9		8	6	2	
		9			1		8	5
8	4	6	3		2			
2			7	9				
	7	8			5	2		
				2	6	7		

GRID - 58

		7				6	1	2
5					6			
8		6	3			4	5	9
	5			3			9	6
	6		1	8				7
		9			2	3		1
	2		6				7	8
	7			9	1	2		4
4		8				1	6	5

GRID - 59

3	6	8	5				4	
		5		2	4		6	8
				8	6	9		1
2		3	4	9	1		8	
	8	9				1	3	
	1	6		5				
	5						1	3
8					5			
		4	1	7	8		9	2

GRID - 60

9	2					5	7	3
		8		3		6		
4	3		5		2	8		1
		1	4	8	9			5
3					6		4	
	5	4	3		1		8	
1				9	8			2
	7	5	1		3			9
			7	4				

GRID - 61

Hard

6			9			1	7	
9	7				8		4	5
		5		1		9		6
7		9		8	4	5	6	
		4		6				
5		3					1	4
	5				3			
4	3			9		6	5	1
			1	5	6		8	3

GRID - 62

Hard

5					2	9	4	3
		4		6			5	1
1		3	9					
9	6	7	1	3	5	4		2
8	3	2	6	4			1	
			8		7			6
			5	7	3			
3								
2				9		6	3	8

GRID - 63

Hard

6	5					9	8	1
4	1	7	3	8		5	6	2
2		9			5	3		4
8	7	6		3				
			8	9	6			
		1	5			8	4	
				6	3	4	9	8
1		8			4	7	2	
3	9	4	2	7			1	

GRID - 64

Hard

			6	3	5		4	
3	4		2	1	7	8		
		5	9	8	4		2	
8			3	2		5		
2				5				6
5	6		4	9			8	2
		9	1	6		7		8
7	5					2		
			5	7			3	9

GRID - 65

Hard

9							3	
		3	7	5	1		2	
		5				4		
7				3		5		6
3		6	1				4	2
8	2					7	9	3
6	3	4	8		5	2		9
2	1				7			4
5		7	4		3			

GRID - 66

Hard

		3			9			
		8	9		6			7
		1	6			5		
8	5	1				6		
6	9		2			7		
	7	3		5		4	8	1
5	6	7		2	3	1	4	8
			1	6	7		5	
	1	9		7				

GRID - 67

4					8		3	2
		3	1	2				9
	2	6	4	3	9			
1	7	9	6			5	3	
5	8	4	3			2	6	9
		2	8				4	
				1	3			
		8					7	
3	1			9		4	2	

GRID - 68

	8				2		4	
		6						2
2		1	5			7		
		6	8		5			4
4	5	2			9	3	6	
			6	4	2			
6		7	2	5	1	9		
	3	9	4	8	7	5		
		5				4	7	1

GRID - 69

1	9	4						5
5	6		4	1	2	9		
7	2	3			8	6	1	
4	5	2			6		9	7
			3		7			
9	3		2				6	
6			8	7				
3	8			2	4			
2		9		1				

GRID - 70

	4	9			1	8	7	
		6			4		3	
3	2		8			5	4	6
9	3		4		5	6	2	
				8	2			
	1		6				5	4
	6		1		8	3		
2			5	3	9			
1	9		7	4			8	5

GRID - 71

1		7	5	6		4		
	5	8	4				1	2
		2		8	3		5	7
		9	6					1
2		3		9			6	4
5				2	1		8	
9		5	2					
	4	6		1				3
3				4		9	7	

GRID - 72

					8	6	4	
8		6						2
3	2	4	7			9	1	
7		2		9	1		5	
9	8			2	3	1	7	
4				5	7			
			3	8	2		9	7
		9	1	7	6	2		
2	7							

GRID - 73

Hard

		9		7	2		4	
5	2	7				3		1
			5	9		7		8
4	6					5	1	9
7	8	3	1		9			
				2	6			7
	9	5	2		8			
2	3		9	1				
1			6			9		2

GRID - 74

Hard

8		7	9		2			6
	6	1			4			9
	3			6	8		7	
	7	6	2			9		4
	8		4		5		6	
	4		6		3	7		8
	2		8	5			4	
	9	8					2	
4		5			6	8	9	

GRID - 75

Hard

8	9	7	3		4		1	
	2				5	8		6
3					2	9	4	7
4	6	1	2		3			8
7			6			3	2	
2		5			8		9	
			1		6			
	4	3	5	2	7			
		8			9			

GRID - 76

Hard

	5		4		1	8	3	
			5	9	8	6	2	
6		8	3	7		4		
3		1	2	5		7	8	9
	8	7		1				
5						1	6	
7	4							
8		5	1					
1	3	9	7					4

GRID - 77

Hard

		5	8	4		3		
	7	3	9	1	6			
2	4	1		3	7	6		
			6		1			
9				5	4	1	8	
	1	6		8		2		5
		4			5		2	1
	5					7	6	
	8		1	6				4

GRID - 78

Hard

				8	9	4	2	
9	5		7		4	6	3	
		2	1	3	6			
2	1				8		4	3
	9	5	3		2			
3				1			5	
	3	6	8		5			
			4	6				
5	4	8			1	3	9	6

ANSWERS

QUIZ

QUESTION 1: B) UNITED KINGDOM

QUESTION 2: C) UNICORN

QUESTION 3: A) HIPPOPOTOMONSTROSESQUIPEDALIOPHOBIA

QUESTION 4: A) SWEDEN

QUESTION 5: A) CAMEL

QUESTION 6: B) ARCHERY

QUESTION 7: B) MARS

QUESTION 8: B) 206

QUESTION 9: A) MALDIVES

QUESTION 10: C) FLAMBOYANCE

QUESTION 11: C) 3

QUESTION 12: A) AUSTRALIA

QUESTION 13: C) STAPES

QUESTION 14: B) SUMO WRESTLING

QUESTION 15: A) THAILAND

QUESTION 16: B) MURDER

QUESTION 17: C) PISA

QUESTION 18: B) KOALAS

QUESTION 19: B) 8

QUESTION 20: C) SNAIL

WORDSEARCH

~~PEE~~	~~POOP~~	~~STINK~~
~~PISS~~	~~SHIT~~	~~STUNK~~
~~URINE~~	~~CRAP~~	~~GROSS~~
~~WEEWEE~~	~~DOODOO~~	~~YUCKY~~
~~WETSEAT~~	~~FLOATERS~~	~~GAG~~

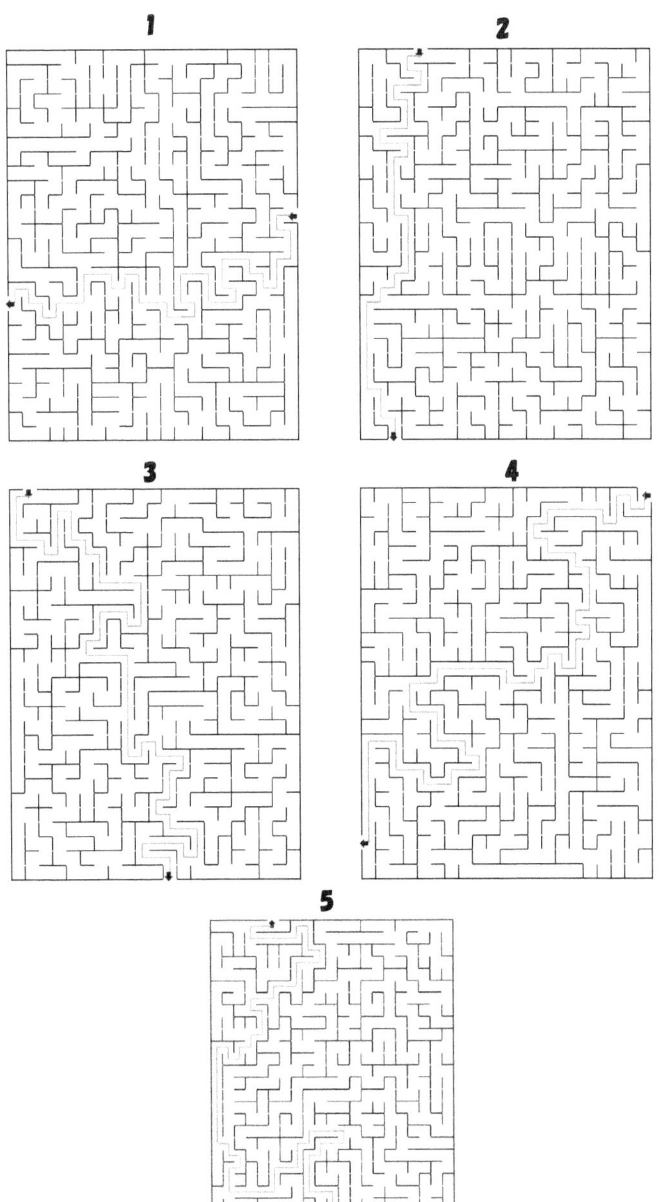

71

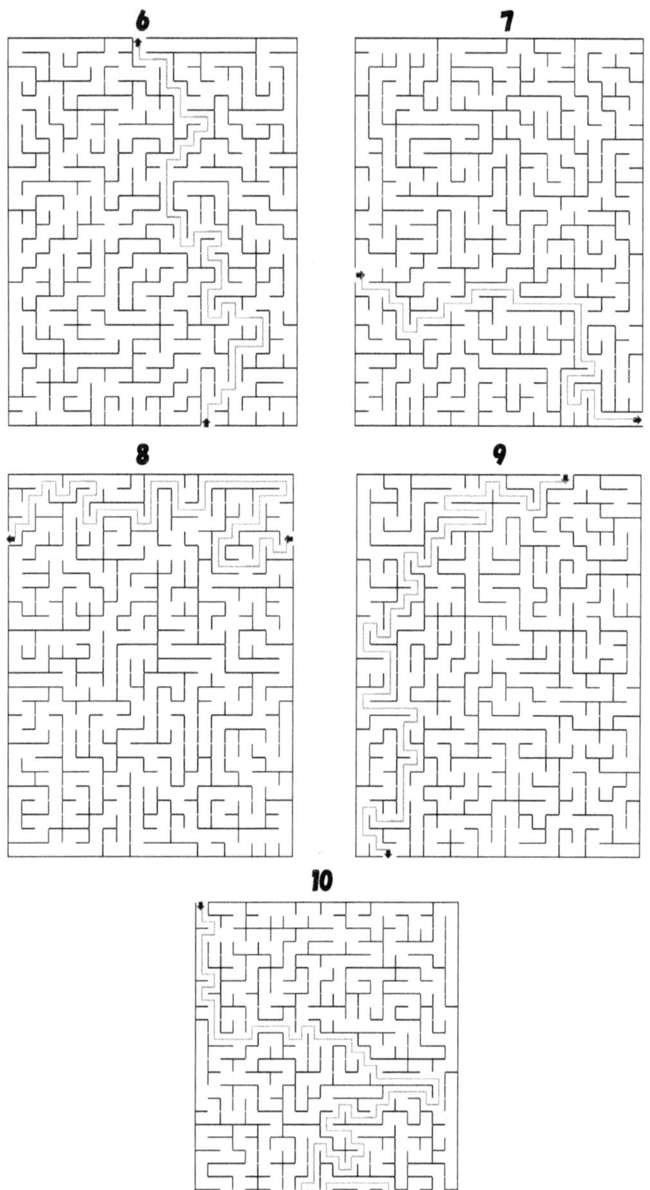

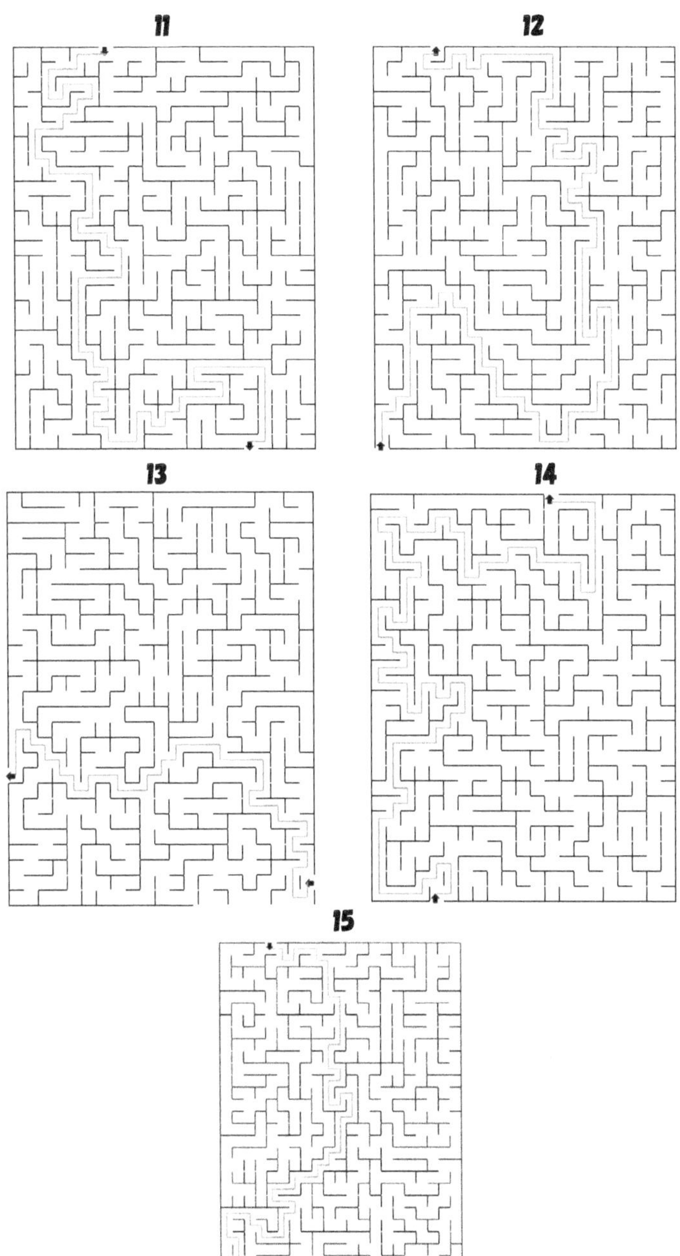

11
12
13
14
15

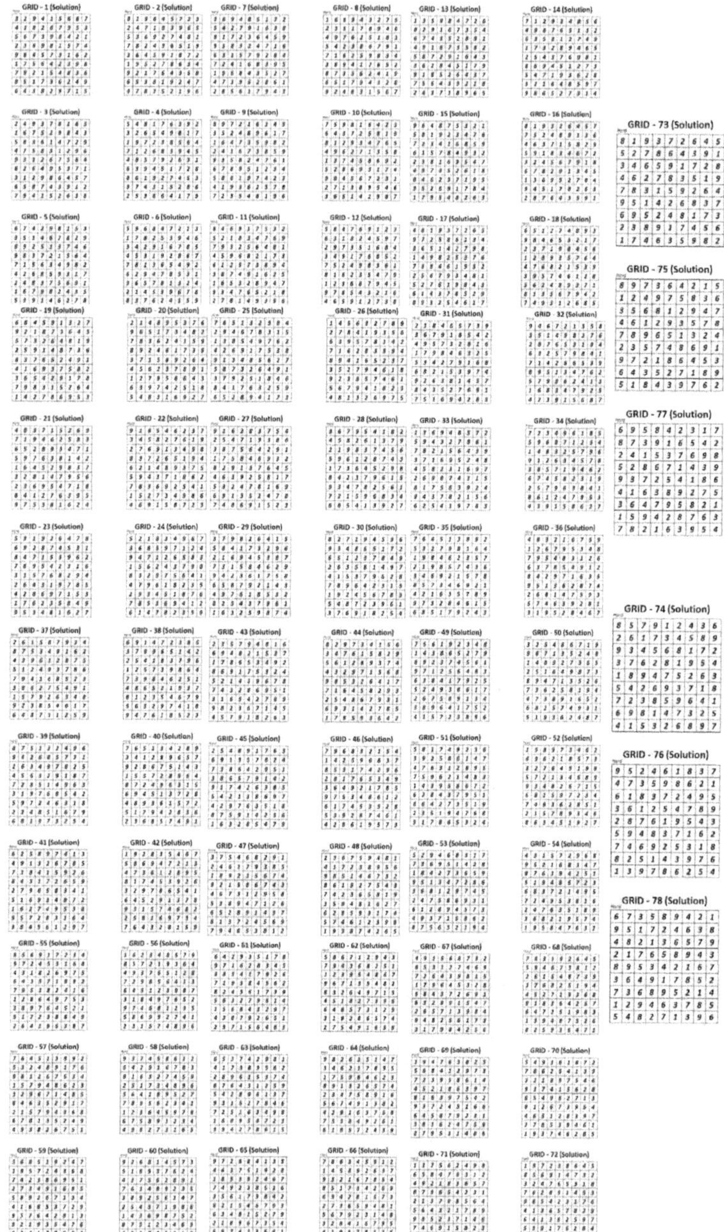

YOU'VE REACHED THE END OF THIS WHACKY, WEIRD, AND WONDERFUL BOOK OF TRIVIA AND FACTS. BUT BEFORE YOU GO, JUST REMEMBER, IF YOU MANAGED TO READ THROUGH ALL OF THIS AND ARE STILL COMFORTABLY SEATED, WELL, I MUST SAY, IT SEEMS LIKE YOU MIGHT HAVE SOME EXPLAINING TO DO IF SOMEONE ASKS WHY YOU TOOK SO LONG IN THERE.

BUT HEY, LET'S FACE IT, IN THE GRAND SCHEME OF THINGS, LEARNING A FEW MIND-BLOWING FACTS AND CHUCKLING AT SOME TOILET HUMOR IS TIME WELL SPENT.

SO, UNTIL OUR NEXT JOURNEY OF KNOWLEDGE, KEEP BEING CURIOUS AND EMBRACING THOSE MOMENTS OF 'BRAIN EXERCISE' THAT ONLY HAPPEN IN THE MOST PRIVATE OF PLACES. HAPPY READING AND... WELL, YOU KNOW, HAPPY SITTING!

www.ingramcontent.com/pod-product-compliance
Lightning Source LLC
Chambersburg PA
CBHW061015260726
48661CB00005B/2195